POETRY OF THE PENIS

A collection of phallic prose.

Compiled by Chelsea Cox

The penile poetry within this book is copyright
© Chelsea Cox
All rights reserved.
First Published in 2023

Front cover image:
The Cerne Abbas Giant, Dorset, England

CONTENTS

Phallus Chronicles: Unveiling the Penile Prowess	5
A Poem of Ardent Awakening	6
The Essence of Climactic Release	7
The "Helicopter"	8
Of Euphemisms and Laughter	9
Phallus Unveiled	9
Fifty Shades of Penis	10
Foreskin or not for skin? That is the question.	12
A Tale of Unexpected Exposure	13
Little Willy, Mighty Heart	13
Conundrum of the Penis	14
Penis Shorts	15
The Biologist's Verse	16
Tale of a Silly Willy	17
Mull of Kintyre	18
The Nilly Willy	20
Penis, dear, penis	21
Limericks of the Penis	22
The Cerne Abbas Giant Unleashed	23
Fearfully and Wonderfully Made	24

Phallus Chronicles: Unveiling the Penile Prowess

Through written prose, come and explore:
An organ unique, and do not ignore
this symbol of strength, in all its might.
A source of delight, both day and night....

    ... THE PENIS!

The penis, my dear, what a curious friend!
The pleasure it brings, from beginning to end.
Oh, wondrous penis, with vigour untold,
A pillar of excitement, immense and bold.
It stands tall and proud, a column of pride,
A marvel of nature - in which we confide.

The penis, my dear, in forms short and long,
Yet each holds a tale - a story or song.
From ancient statues, to jokes that roam,
Or hen-party giggles, and art of poem.
A spring of joy and connection so true,
Intimacy's dance, and treasures anew.

A Poem of Ardent Awakening

Hark! Witness the member, part of man's guise,
A tender fragment of nature's devise.
Whilst oft at rest in tranquil slumber's keep,
In passion's clasp, it doth with ardour leap.

As Cupid's dart pierces deep the heart's core,
The crimson tide surges, through veins it does pour.
And lo! The shaft rises in a regal array.
A flag unfurled, in sentiment's grand ballet.

'Tis not mere flesh, but human desire,
Love, and romance, and hearts set afire.
With zeal, and vigour, the longplum stands tall,
In fiery spirit, he hath answered the call.

The Essence of Climactic Release

When a man reaches the peak of sexual stimulation,
Ejaculation occurs, a natural culmination.
It begins with sensations, intense and profound,
As pleasure builds up, spreading all around.
Muscles within his body respond,
Contracting rhythmically, a phenomenon beyond.

The seminal vesicles and prostate gland,
Release their fluids, to your command.
These fluids, along with spermatozoa, unite,
Forming semen - a substance of sticky might.
Traveling through the urethra at speed.
Climax emerges, a conclusion indeed!

The "Helicopter"

In a world of whimsy and joyful delight,
Imagine the aircraft taking to flight.
A cylindrical wonder, meaty and long,
With playful imagination, let's join along.

Watch as the chopper takes to the air,
Spinning and hovering with frisky flair.
Its meaty propulsion, a hilarious sight,
As it hovers and spins, giving delight.

Happy laughter fills the jolly scene,
As the "sausage-copter" performs with a sheen.
Up and down it bounces, in the lively endeavour,
Bringing joy and mirth, a memory to treasure.

With each spin, it wobbles, defying all norms,
A makeshift 'copter, with tasty transforms.
In the world of pleasure, laughter resounds,
A silly spectacle, where happiness abounds.

Of Euphemisms and Laughter

The Pecker, the Rod, the One-eyed Snake,
Their names may make us giggle or shake.
Shlong, Willy, Dong, or Member,
Each a name, a part to remember.
Joystick, Ding-a-ling, Chopper and Cock.
Names to bring laughter, smile and shock.

Phallus Unveiled

        Penile pleasure,
      On**e** eyed monster
   ding-a-li**n**g
      d**i**ck
        shlong

Fifty Shades of Penis

In the realm of passion, and artistic hue,
An ingenious canvas, where desire breaks through.
"Fifty Shades of Penis," a colourful display,
So come and journey along this way.

In the first shade, a whisper of anticipation,
An erotic sonnet, a sensual foundation.
With metaphors and imagery, yearning ignites,
Intricately woven verses, intimate delights.

The second shade, a brushstroke of devotion,
A lyrical ballad, a rhythmic motion.
Words interlace, like bodies in dance,
Expressing ardour, in every poetic stance.

The third shade, a mosaic of cherished desires,
A tapestry of endurance, as craving transpires.
Sensuous images, a wordplay so fine,
Capturing the essence of love's design.

The fourth shade, an abstract expression,
Embracing contrasts, exploring obsession.
Verses intertwine, like bodies intertwined,
A graceful exploration, the sacred and refined.

The fifth shade, a haiku's delicate grace,
Conveying longing, in brevity's embrace.
Syllables unite, like lovers in the night,
Evoking passion, in each line's delight.

From shades one to fifty, a kaleidoscope unfurls,
Creative expressions, where intimacy twirls.
Innovative styles, and imaginative scenes,
An expressive symphony, of phallic means.

So let the words flow, in colours diverse,
Celebrating the willy, with poetic verse.
In "Fifty Shades of Penis," let the longplum shine,
In the canvass of love, an artistic design.

Foreskin or not for skin? That is the question.

Foreskin of not for skin? Let's now begin,
To explore the divergent realms within.
In one, a cover, protective and kind,
Preserving sensations, a pleasure to find.

On the other, revealed, a different display,
Unveiling the bell, in a distinctive way.
Smooth and exposed, a sight to behold,
With sensitivity remaining, as stories unfold.

These contrasts in form, unique and true,
Showcasing the marvels of what bodies can do.
Diverse expressions of pleasure and delight,
Embracing the variations, shining in their own light.

A Tale of Unexpected Exposure

So, my fella thought he'd get some shorts,
But boy, oh boy, they were way too damn short!
His willy popped out, it was so embarrassing,
People cracked up and wouldn't stop laughing!

Embarrassed as hell, he tried to hide,
While everyone around just laughed, wide-eyed.
Now he keeps those short shorts out of sight,
Only for bedroom fun, when we're alone at night.

Little Willy, Mighty Heart

Once upon a time, in a land far away,
Lived a man with a smile that brightened each day.
He carried a secret, a tale to be told,
About his body, unique and bold.

For this man possessed a rather small willy.
A one-inch-wonder, but he didn't feel silly.
He knew only true worth lay in his heart,
And that beauty transcends the physical part.

He shared his wisdom with those feeling down,
Spreading the message across the town:
"Love your willy, just as you are,
For confidence shines, like a radiant star."

Conundrum of the Penis

Q-S-E-I-F-P-N-I-B

As the famous clock's music reaches its final phase,
the presenter beckons with an elated gaze.
"Any words?" he chortles, sparking curiosity in the air,
And the contestants brace themselves, ready to dare.
The first, forlorn, proclaims "FINE" - a four-letter feat.
A simple word - yet innocent and neat.

But the second contestant, with a gleam in her eye,
delights in the unexpected, ready to reply.
"I've got a five," she exclaims, mischievous and sly,
"The word is PENIS".
                   The studio resounds in a joyous cry.
Laughter ripples through the crowd, giggles rise,
at the startling twist - the linguistic surprise.

Why does PENIS provoke laughter's embrace?
Not for its inherent nature or societal chase.
But for the innocence disrupted,
               the surprising wordplay,
that brings people together, in a moment's play.
Through humour, we glimpse our shared humanity,
And revel in the joy of linguistic profanity.

Penis Shorts

1.
I stand tall and proud, with a sense of grace,
A vessel of connection, an intimate embrace.
In moments of passion, I come alive,
Bringing pleasure and joy, helping love thrive.

2.
With a joyful swing, it happily sways,
In playful rhythm, a carefree display.
A whimsical dance, full of delight,
Bringing happiness, morning 'til night.

3.
Confined in briefs, I yearn to be free,
To roam untethered, wild and carefree.
Release me from this stifling embrace,
Let me find freedom, my rightful space.

The Biologist's Verse

A vital part of the male anatomy,
The penis! A fascinating entity.
Its structure is a wonder to explore,
And so, let's delve into its physical core.

At the base, the root holds its place,
With blood vessels, nerves, and space.
The shaft extends, erect or at ease,
Covered by skin, sensations to please.

The glans, the tip, a sensitive site,
Has countless nerve endings, delighting in light.
The urethral opening, where everything flows,
And during arousal, semen it bestows.

Beneath the skin, two chambers reside,
Corpora cavernosa, side by side.
These spongy tissues, when filled with blood,
Cause an erection, strong and proud.

The frenulum, a delicate band,
Connects the glans to the shaft, hand in hand.
And on the underside, a ridge may appear,
Called the corona, adding charm and sheer.

Within each verse, we've traversed the terrain,
Unveiling the wonders of this bodily domain.
From the base to the tip, a captivating form,
The penis stands tall, weathering every storm.

Tale of a Silly Willy

There once was a silly willy
Whose head was quite full of silly.
He thought he could fly,
With a broomstick up high,
But he only crashed in Mississippi.

The silly willy was sad,
He thought he was bad,
But his good lady said,
"Don't be silly, instead,
Just try again, and be glad."

So the silly willy tried again,
And this time he didn't crash.
He flew through the air,
And landed without a care,
And he was so happy, and glad.

The silly willy was a hero,
He had learned to fly.
And he was so joyful,
For he knew he could do anything,
If he just tried, and didn't be silly.

Mull of Kintyre

Oh, Mull of Kintyre, where passions ignite,
A landscape of joy and anticipation's light.
Where rugged hills meet the boundless sea,
A place where sentiment soars and spirits roam free.

The whispering winds carry tales of old,
Of a land so enchanting, a story untold.
With rolling meadows and heathery moors,
The spirit of Kintyre, forever endures.

In the golden dawn, anticipation thrives,
As the sun paints the landscape, our souls revive.
The air, crisp and pure, fills every breath,
Awakening passions, conquering all depths.

Oh, Mull of Kintyre, where dreams take flight,
In the soft twilight, under stars so bright.
The melody of laughter echoes through the glen,
As merriment and music intertwine, again and again.

A tapestry of joy weaves its vibrant hue,
In the hearts of those who call Kintyre true.
With each step on the land, with every embrace,
Passion ignites, leaving no trace of space.

The sea sings a song, with waves that caress,
Inviting adventure, a tender embrace.
In the depths of its waters, secrets lie,
In the dance of passion, where desires amplify.

Oh, Mull of Kintyre, a place so divine,
A haven for love, where spirits align.
In the arms of its beauty, we find our grace,
A sanctuary of joy, in this magical place.

The Mull of Kintyre marks Scotland's southwestern tip. The 'Mull of Kintyre test' is thought to be employed by the British Board of Film Classification to evaluate the permissibility of depicting an erect penis, taking into account its angle in relation to the peninsula on maps.

The Nilly Willy

In shadows cast by a lingering gloom,
A tale unfolds of a man's inner room.
Where once stood strength and vigorous might,
A cloud now veils his passionate light.
A floppy frustration, a limp weight to bear,
But within this struggle, a dream lingers there.

Amidst the trials and doubts which abide,
Love - and understanding - stand strong beside.
A partner's embrace, supportive and kind,
Shines beacons of hope, with warmth intertwined.
Seeking counsel, they venture to find,
Solutions and treatments that fate may bind.

Throughout this odyssey of hearts laid bare,
Is discovered a love and joy beyond compare.
With patience and perseverance, they embark,
On a journey of connection, in love's own arc.
Together they navigate passion's vast sea,
United in purpose, forever to be.

Penis, dear, penis

Penis, dear, penis

In your presence I am at peace,
With the world far from our sight,
In this moment, time recedes.

Your touch is gentle, yet strong,
Your head is soft and sweet,
Your shaft is warm within my skin,
And I am lost in your heat.

I open my eyes for a ventral view,
In a wave of passion and desire,
At this time, there is no past,
No future, only now.

Penis, dear, penis.
Under your veins, I am home.

Limericks of the Penis:

There once was a fellow named Dennis,
Whose pride was his manhood, tremendous.
With a confident sway,
He'd go on his way,
Bringing smiles to all who bore witness

There once was a lad full of cheer,
Whose member brought him no fear.
Though not huge or grand,
He'd lend a helping hand,
Bringing pleasure and laughter, my dear.

In the bedroom of bliss and delight,
There's a tale of an organ upright.
With passion it would rise,
To the awe of her eyes,
A symbol of zeal burning bright.

There once was a bodily function,
With a visual and pleasurable junction.
With contractions and force,
Semen took its course,
In a whitish and sticky eruption.

The Cerne Abbas Giant Unleashed

In a land of ancient lore and pride,
I, the Cerne Abbas Giant, stand tall and wide.
A chalk figure, a symbol of fertility,
A massive erection, for all to see.

But alas, a cheese company came my way,
Printing my image on their product, they say.
Yet, they dared to omit my vital part,
My proud manhood, they removed with "art".

The cheesy directors defended their deed,
Using my censored appendage, indeed.
But a supermarket, with their request so strange,
Demanded trousers for me, a prudish change.

Oh, Oxford cheese makers, you caused dismay,
To deface a national monument, I must say,
A disgraceful act to sell your smelly cheese,
Disrespecting heritage with such ease!

Oh, I, the Cerne Abbas Giant, stand tall,
A mark of power, fertility, and all.
In this tumultuous tale of prudery and shame,
I yearn for my penis forever to remain.

The Cerne Abas Giant is pictured on the front of this book.
As reported by the Dorset Echo, a Cheesemaker censored this
famous giant's manhood in May 2023.
dorsetecho.co.uk/news/23562157
.cheese-company-castrates-dorsets-cerne-abbas-giant

Fearfully and Wonderfully Made

"Fearfully and wonderfully made!"
Each part of the body, a masterpiece laid.
From head to toe, in intricate design,
A symphony of creation, thus divine.

In sophisticated folds of the skin,
The wonders of life do begin.
From eyes that perceive the world's array,
To hands that shape it, day by day.

The heart, a steady rhythm, beats,
With every pulse, life's journey greets.
The lungs, a delicate dance of breath,
As life's concerto finds its graceful breadth.

Muscles that move, strength they hold,
Bones that support, a framework bold.
Nerves that transmit, sensations ignite,
Connecting body and soul, day and night.

And yes, even the intimate part,
Fearfully and wonderfully made, as of art.
A vessel of pleasure, a symbol of connection,
A testament to the body's reflection.

For in the tapestry of the human form,
All parts are significant, and there is no norm.
Each contributes to the whole, you see,
A masterpiece of creation: Fearfully and wonderfully.

Made in the USA
Columbia, SC
02 May 2025